For Janice
From Gemma and
Teddy Hoskins

Teddy Tales
A Puppy Primer

by
Gemma Hoskins, a lady
and Teddy Hoskins, her dog

ISBN 978-1-62806-327-1 (print | hardback)

Library of Congress Control Number 2021916765

Published by Salt Water Media
29 Broad Street, Suite 104
Berlin, MD 21811
www.saltwatermedia.com

Cover art by Maria Staub Goebel; interior images used with permission from the author, Maria Staub Goebel, Kinsey LeBrun, Linda Williams, Trucie Petty, Anne Meyers Copeland, Viki Honeywell, Sharon Bush, Sasha Gardner, and Sammy Morgan.

This book is dedicated to dog lovers, young and old, especially those lucky folks who are learning how to be dog parents for the first time.

Introduction

When I was a kid growing up in the 50s and 60s, we lived in the West Hills suburb of West Baltimore. I don't remember anyone actually walking a dog. Dogs then and there just sort of ran around the neighborhood and playground loose, with all the kids just sort of running around the neighborhood and playground loose, too. If someone had a dog on

a leash, we most likely thought it was dangerous and were probably told by our parents to stay away from it.

There were two big fun dogs that were around every day – Rob Atwood's Duke, a sort of boxer I think, and Jerry Pointac's Hansel, which we all pronounced as if there was a short O in place of the short A. "Hansel" rhymed with Tonsil.

The man next door in our row houses, Mr. Kemp, had a big black Doberman named Ginger that scared us so much that we did not walk down the sidewalk in the backyard because it ran along the Kemp's sidewalk in their backyard. Ginger's nose could reach over the metal fence between our yards. She barked and growled at us. Taking the trash out was terrifying. Mr. Kemp called the dog "Ginja", rhyming it with ninja, before there were even any of those. Like he was from Boston or someplace fancy. The Kemps were definitely not fancy. I think Mr. Kemp knew when we were going out to play in our yard or walk to the gate and would send 'Ginja' out there to snarl at us. I never saw that dog anyplace else but in that backyard. Kind of sad. For the dog.

I don't know if I was afraid of other dogs or sort of neutral. Duke and Hansel don't count, because they were part of our gang. We probably tried to ride them or get them to pull our wagons and sleds. I think nervous, yappy or fast dogs made me a little uncomfortable. My brother Jim was walking home from school one day, when, about a block away, a dog ran after him. Jim jumped up on top of a Volkswagen Beetle. The dog jumped up there too and took a chunk out of Jim's leg, right through his school uniform pants. So, I don't think Jim likes dogs, any dogs, even to this day and he is an old man. With a scar on his leg. A very big scar.

So, that said, this book is about my first dog, my Teddy. Now mind you, I am no spring chicken. Teddy came to live with me when I was 59 years old. To say a dog was on my bucket list sounds petty and trite, just something to try or do. But Teddy IS my bucket list and I love almost every inch of him. There are a few inches I do not love and am in denial about, as you will see.

There are poems and stories here, but also lessons I have learned or made up in becoming a dog mom. I hope that you will find it fun and funny, practical and impractical. Most of all I hope that you will find a place in your heart for Teddy, the cutest little manny-man that ever peed on anyone's lawn. And maybe you will think about finding a dog to fill your own life with chaos, cuddles and surprises.

Love and barks from
Gemma and Teddy Hoskins

A Dog-Barking Poem

A dog barking at night
has a lonely, 1950's backyard-at-night-in-rowhouses
feel to it.
Incandescent lights that fade into dark black yards and alleys.
That one bark, (if I wait any night, I will hear it)
takes me back to someplace I knew but was not in. –
Someplace outside of my cozy house
in somebody else's concrete airy-way.
It would be the same Lady and the Tramp sort of dog.
It has never really changed.

Kinsey LeBrun

In the Beginning

In the fall of 2010, I went with the "let's-try-to be-friends" ex-guy-person to a party on a windfarm. He was a bass guitar player, and I was going to sit under a tree and drink wine and take pictures of the band, which was not even a band, just a bunch of old guys with guitars and one had a good voice. I actually was trying to not smell the stink bugs that were raining down, pouring off the trees and whipping around my head and face.

Into my field of vision came the most stunning and unusual dog I had ever seen. Fleecy like a lamb, legs like uncooked spaghetti...pasta legs, and a stuffed animal face like a bear. Bailing on my photo job immediately, I ventured off to find out who owned this creature and what it was. That was the day I fell in love again – with labradoodles, not the guy-person.

Arriving home, I could not stop thinking about that dog. Maybe I would get one. Yeah, that's what I would do. Turning on the TV as I do as soon as I come into the house, (it was my roommate) I was delightfully surprised to see on the pet channel a program already in progress on guess what? – Labradoodles. It was fate. I decided that day.

Kinsey LeBrun

Searching

I had never had a dog before, but I sure knew how to use a computer. With luck again on my side, I found a breeder no more than a half hour from my home. Waltzing Matilda's Australian Labradoodles. I spent hours looking at the website, dreaming all winter about those dogs. I just had to do this...

In May, I finally took the plunge and applied for a puppy with Michelle Walker, the breeder-lady on the site pix with all those dogs laying on top of her on her couch looking really happy and warm. I learned that, in order to reserve a dog, I would need to complete an 8-page application that asked me everything but what kind of milk I drank. Oh yes, and the $500 deposit...did I mention that? Deposit. What was the price tag on this creature? Oh my...$3500. The cost of my last trip to New Zealand. 4 mortgage payments. Part of a car, braces for my teeth. A dog. A dog that I could play with and love and keep for my very own. I did it.

Waiting

I was not able to meet or even see my dog until pick-up day. Now understand, at the time of my application, the dog had not even been conceived yet. I picked the litter I wanted: the parents were Sadie Soleil and Hobson's Choice. Labradoodles are a cross between a Labrador retriever and a poodle. Teddy's mom and dad and all his grand- and great-grandparents were also labradoodles. Some of you will shame me for getting a designer dog and not a rescue. That's okay. You be you and I'll be me. We all spend money in different ways, right?

So, Sadie and Hobson sort of looked red. I wanted red. I said I want a red little boy. What? Michelle picks the dog for me? Dern, that stinks.

Here are Sadie and Hobson, probably before they got together. They look too demure to have already done it...

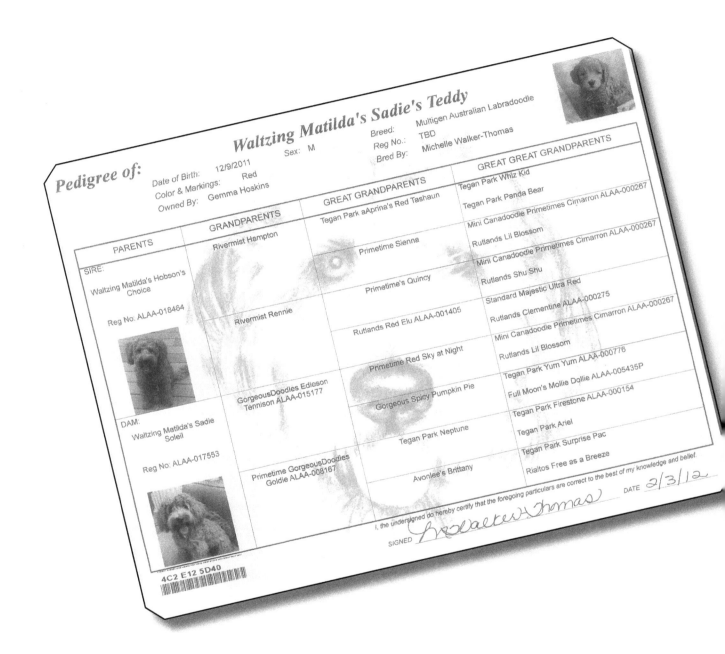

Pedigree of: *Waltzing Matilda's Sadie's Teddy*

Date of Birth: 12/9/2011
Color & Markings: Red
Owned By: Gemma Hoskins

Sex: M
Breed: Multigen Australian Labradoodle
Reg No.: TBD
Bred By: Michelle Walker-Thomas

PARENTS	GRANDPARENTS	GREAT GRANDPARENTS	GREAT GREAT GRANDPARENTS
SIRE: Waltzing Matilda's Hobson's Choice	Rivermist Hampton	Tegan Park aAprina's Red Tashaun	Tegan Park Whiz Kid
			Tegan Park Panda Bear
		Primetime Sienna	Mini Canadoodle Primetimes Cimarron ALAA-000267
			Rutlands Lil Blossom
Reg No: ALAA-018464	Rivermist Rennie	Primetime's Quincy	Mini Canadoodle Primetimes Cimarron ALAA-000267
			Rutlands Shu Shu
		Rutlands Red Elu ALAA-001405	Standard Majestic Ultra Red
			Rutlands Clementine ALAA-000275
DAM: Waltzing Matilda's Sadie Soleil	GorgeousDoodles Edleson Tennison ALAA-015177	Primetime Red Sky at Night	Rutlands Clementine ALAA-000267
			Rutlands Lil Blossom
		Gorgeous Spicy Pumpkin Pie	Tegan Park Yum Yum ALAA-000776
			Full Moon's Mollie Dollie ALAA-005435P
Reg No: ALAA-017553	Primetime GorgeousDoodles Goldie ALAA-008167	Tegan Park Neptune	Tegan Park Firestone ALAA-000154
			Tegan Park Ariel
		Avonlee's Brittany	Tegan Park Surprise Pac
			Rialtos Free as a Breeze

I, the undersigned do hereby certify that the foregoing particulars are correct to the best of my knowledge and belief.

SIGNED *Walter Thomas*   DATE 2/3/12

4C2 E12 5D40

Starters: Pre-Puppy Homework

What does it really mean to get your house ready for your new arrival?

- Lay on the floor sort of at puppy eye-level.
- Ignore the dust under the china closet and hall stand. That is a different project. Called housekeeping. This is dogkeeping.
- Now move everything on this list at least five feet off the ground:

Your knitting, your crossword puzzle books. pens, pennies, pencils, paper clips, papers, newspapers, slippers, shoes, socks, underpants, sweatshirts, purses, bookbags, knapsacks, shells from your trip to Cape Cod, library books, houseplants, coupons, keys, phones, belts, hats, gloves and scarves, jewelry, your MP3 player, false teeth, retainers, and the checkbook. Regardless of how conscientious you are at this stage, inevitably anything you own in pairs like gloves and earrings is going to end up alone. Get used to wearing a red mitten with your black leather driving glove, a green leg warmer with a striped trouser sock.

- This will probably take you the better part of the afternoon, so when you finish get back down on the floor with a glass of wine and a straw and double check.
- Next, get some good old masking tape. If you are a teacher or married to one, you know where to get it on short notice. Tape all your electric cords up the wall, yes, right on your Sherwin Williams eggshell-finish buttered popcorn walls. Mind you, from the outlet all the way to the appliance. You can and will do this. Electric tape is too black and will offend your fashion sense every time you enter the room. Stick with masking tape.
- Under your computer table are cords, lots of cords. Put a shoe box under there as far back as you can reach. Poke a hole in the lid and shove all those cords thru the hole and into the box. Tape the lid closed. Now take a cou-

ple of old vinyl album covers, like the Partridge Family or Barry Manilow but not Brian Wilson and not the Beatles. Or Pink Floyd. Place the covers in front of all that and hope for the best. Good luck if you have to mess with the cords for some reason.

- A fireplace grate is not a good dog gate. Need I say more? Because it is in three sections it certainly fits the door space but a wee shove from a dog and there goes your toes and his nose, the door frame and the hardwood floor. Get a baby gate, no, get two. And keep reading.

Kinsey LeBrun

My dog has more living space than I do...

Teddy lived in the kitchen for a long time. As long as it took for me not to be afraid of him. I installed a baby gate between the dining room and kitchen and a dog door in the sliding glass door to my back deck. This gave him access to the deck and the back yard. Later when I installed a dog door in the walk out basement slider, and another baby gate at the top of the basement steps, he was living big. If you can picture this, good on you. Now he goes wherever and everywhere. Because now we are buddies.

 14

Milk Teeth Hurt...

Those damn little sharp shark teeth of Teddy's made me have to wear long sleeves so no one would see all the marks on my arms. I looked like a heroin addict. I cried. He bit. I said No. He mouthed me constantly. I hated my dog for a few minutes and then I went to work on this. A squirt bottle, no good. Holding his mouth closed, even worse. Ouch. Swaddling him, forget it. He's not the Baby Jesus. Yelping like a hurt dog, he yelped back. Replacing my arm with a toy. He is not stupid. Putting him in a crate, now he is crying and barking. Walking away made me feel like an unfinished failure. The answer? TIME. Teddy needed time and so did I. Now I have to put up with kisses, but my arms are looking awesome especially with a tan and a few days at the gym.

Kinsey LeBrun

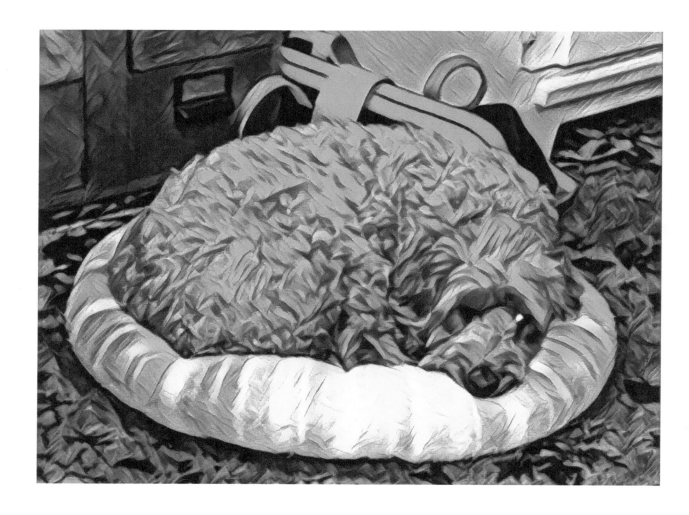

Teddy sleeps on my bed. ALL of my bed...

On one of our trips to the vet, I asked the doctor what she thought about dogs sleeping with owners. Her answer made me think. "If you do it, make sure it is for you, not him. Don't let him get used to it. You will have to do it every night." Needless to say, Teddy sleeps with me every night. The first time, I felt creepy about it. Like this little critter with farts and bad breath was wiggling around in the dark. I left a light on all night. I was afraid of him. I did not get a good night's sleep. But the next morning, there was his little bear face staring right in my eyes. Waiting for me to do something. He was barely able to go up and down the steps, much less jump up on the bed which is very high.

For a while, Teddy would waddle up the staircase and stand next to the bed looking at me. I would pick him up and say, "Fly, Teddy, Fly!" and plop him right down on his spot. He never stayed in his spot. He stayed in my spot. I was often falling off the edge of the mattress clinging to the sheets for life. Teddy stayed on the bed with me for a few hours. When he began to whimper, I knew he needed to go outside and pee. When we returned, he waited expectantly for me, his mom. This time he rolled over and shoved his back and butt against mine. This was nice. I could do without a big blanket. He would touch his nose to my hand, and I fell asleep stroking his little curly head like he was a doll.

After a while, Teddy figured out that if he took a running start from the hallway, and across my bedroom, he could leap up onto the bed by himself. I almost cried when I realized he did not need his mom to put him to bed any more.

Nine years later, I still sleep with my Teddy. He is much bigger but still keeps me warm and cozy. Now in the house where I live, there is no room for Teddy to get a running start to fly up on the bed. We tried steps, a doggy bed, blankets and a bench. The bed is very high, hard for even me to climb up there. Our process is odd but works. First, I take Ted out to potty before we get in bed. When we return. I slide off his harness and ask him if he is ready to get up. He stands still and lowers his head slightly. I bend over and place my arms under his belly from the side. I count 1, 2, Just before 3, he tenses his muscles and gets ready to be lifted. I still yell "Fly, Teddy fly!" He flies up in my arms and I swing him over onto the bed on 3. Then we spoon. He is the only man I have ever slept with who spoons and does not want anything in return.

Sometimes during the night, Teddy jumps off if I am listening to a book or watching a movie on my tablet. He likes it quiet for sleeping. But when I stop and turn off the light for good, he scurries back to the lift-me-up spot. I go to get him, and he lays down on the floor. Come on, dude. I get back in bed and he does it again. And again. I give up. I go in the guest room and sleep on top of the quilt on the guest twin bed. He can jump up there by himself. The things we do for love. And dogs.

Quandary

Mismatched shoes
Where are their mates?
Pockets full of plastic bags and crumbly bits.
An old but really warm hat
 on my head.
A cardboard box for hiding and breaking the wind.
Waiting...waiting...waiting
I have to pee so bad and it is so cold.
 really cold out here.
No, I am not homeless.
I have a new puppy.

Poopy Toes

Where Teddy pooped,
I did not know
Until I saw it on my toe
It squished between my toes and then
I took a step - it squished again.
I'm in bare feet - how dumb was I
To think I'd walk there clean and dry?
Now how am I to get this shit
Off of my foot each little bit
I hop inside, with foot held up
Behind me trots my little pup.
With foot in sink and water hot
I squirt between my toes a lot.
The poop comes off, goes down the drain
I'll never go barefoot again.

Anne Meyers Copeland

A River Runs Through It

Diversity was the name of our afternoon in Patapsco State Park.

People of every color, shape, age and size.

Dogs of every color, shape, age and size.

Breeds galore.

Oodles of doodles - goldendoodles, labradoodles, schnoodles, cockapoodles, schitzoo-dles. Wheels of every color, shape, age and size - skates, scooters, bikes - tandem, moun-tain,

10 speed, banana.

Feet. Feet, Feet.

A plane drones thru it. A train does too.

What? A baptism! an Easter egg hunt!

Two huge grey geese barking up against the tide.

Teddy barking back.

We pause, we watch

"you can do it!"

What will happen when they reach the falls?

Will they turn back? Will they take to the sky?

Will they do a salmon jump?

Engineers from England, pharmaceutical robot engineers

A Russian girl

We talk dogs and plants

Their seeds have not germinated, tomatoes and corn, gone now.

I tell them in my best master gardener sort of style that it will be ok

if they do it again

in another month.

The swinging bridge - Teddy walks drunk.

The shy park ranger – Teddy wants to shake his paw.

A short rest – 3 gumdrops for Gem's low blood sugar.

We're walking far today.

We refill Teddy's water pouch.

We venture back upstream.

Flashing lights, now traffic cop, all ticketed but me,

The last parked illegally under the railroad bridge.

We run real fast and make our getaway.

Diversity all day save for one organic but ever present living thing

Assaults our every sense.

Changing slowing

Dripping winding

Always there

Kinsey LeBrun

Bedtime Story

There's a dog bone in my bed and a paw atop my head.

For my puppy has just found my cozy nest

He has wiggled in there tight,

He is quite set for the night.

But me? No, I know I'll get no rest.

He will spoon for just a bit, then he'll get right up and sit.

With his muzzle and his breath right in my face

And some kisses he will share and licks all on my hair

Then he'll make his move and take up all my space

And then just when I give in, that dern Teddy-man will spin

He'll go dizzy dizzy til he falls.

He'll be scratching on my spread that I have upon my bed.

(Should have shortened those long nails on Teddys paws)

Kinsey LeBrun

And then Teddy's gone but not for long.

I hear his pawsteps going down the hall.

Now he's padding back on up.

That mischievous little pup

With his blankie, and his own wee teddy bear

So we're back to the game of getting to sleep.

All the toys and we creatures prayers say.

And my buddy's content with his foot in my face

And I'd have it no other way.

So I whisper good night and I hold him real tight.

And I pray that we have many days

Of messes and fun and those licks every one

And he cuddles and in Mom's arms stays.

The Night Ted Ate Paddington

Paddington

Sammy Morgan

Paddington has tiny arms that clip onto my lamp's electric cord. Paddington is two inches tall. He wears a little blue felt coat. His boots are red, and he has a yellow rain hat on his fuzzy head.

Well, he used to have all that. His head is chewed nearly all the way off his neck; half a boot is stuck on half a foot. The other foot is fine but bootless. A scrap of that hat is too far under my bed for me to reach. Teddy had fun.

How could he have known that Paddington is over 30 years old? That I rescued him from the Johns Hopkins Hospital when Ernie was there the very first time and I had to go to the gift shop so that Ernie would not see me cry?

How could Teddy know that Paddington made every trip to the hospital with his Man and clung fiercely to many a call button cord and in fact when he was left behind alone he held on tight knowing that we would drive back to the city to unclip his little arms and bring him safely home?

How could Teddy know that my heart was breaking then and is cracking a wee bit now?

All he knows is that Mommy is sad and probably wants her bears, her little chewed up bear and her real live teddy bear. Paddington lands in my lap. Teddy lands in my lap, thrilled to lick salty wet off my silly face.

Kinsey LeBrun

The Hand That Does Not Change

Mommy and Teddy are waiting to cross. on a Catonsville October windy Sunday
Late afternoon slants thru the trees of the Coldwell Banker corner
But the hand does not change

Mommy pushes the round silver knob that promises access more than once
Teddy barks at trucks as he sits in his wait
But the hand does not change

The 3, count 'em, three tiny little icons, Signs if you will
Tell us what to do
Hand do not cross
Green man, go ahead and start
Red do not start but really hurry up fast, ok?
But the hand doesn't change

Doggie treats (all digestible) in a torn paper sack under Mommy's arm
The wind shifts, her arm does too
The cow trachea (all digestible) slides out
And lands on the curb like a monster skeleton prop for Halloween
But the hand doesn't change

A driver toots as if to tell me it fell and to pick up that awful thing there
Another beeps, he laughs and wrinkles his nose
The third dares us with a honk to disobey the hand.
The hand that does not change

I may be blind, but not that blind
That mean ole man will never know
the smokey taste of peanut-butter-stuffed
cow-trachea that Teddy savors
and still it does not change

Glad we are so darn cute, Teddy and Mom
I know the cars will wait to see what we decide
So we start off the curb into the street.
Left foot first let's go.
Against that stupid hand all lit and orange
Telling me to knock it off
Knowing eyes on us, Mommy tries her best
To be coy and cute and a good, no great dog owner

We reach our destination
We did not die, we did not fall,
We hate that hand that did not change

Grandma's Rug and the Beater Bar

This is Grandma's rug

Her really old and really nice Oriental rug

Really red, Grandma's dead

She left it to me many years ago and so it is in my house

With my dog

And his, you-know.

This is Teddy's you-know

He used to not always go outside when it was time to you-know

For some strange and silly reason it did not stink, so the poop on the carpet I did not smell or see until

Vacuuming just on a whim

Not really noticing, just you know vacuuming

That beater bar made little hotdogs and burgers right on the carpet

And mashed pooptatoes in the beaters of the bar in the vacuum

No whirring anymore

Just mumble thuds

Then

Nothing

But

Stinky

What should I do?

What would you do?

Take it apart

Clean it up

Put it back

Uh that would be a big NO

No touching no looking no smelling

Just gloves and a trash bag and a no more beater bar

 28

That smearied serial number

Oh shit, yes shit, no shit

Now we got it

Ordered that bar

That beater bar.

I am so sorry Grandma in heaven forgive me my sin

And lead me into life everlasting with no more rugs and doggy doo.

Kinsey LeBrun

Walking Teddy
November Mist

Through the fog at 5:13 just now was eerily calming. Pools of fuzzy streetlights, dark too soon. A lone far-off cry...a fox on the dune calling her little ones? Even the waves crash softly. A few porch lights left on by a renter or two. But not even the Sunny Vue welcome globe in their front hall is lit. No leaving the light on there. We're moving easy like ghosts. Enjoying our bubble, our connection. A slight tug and Teddy stops. Doing his biz in the shadowy dark mulch. Me cleaning up by feel alone through Food Lion plastic. Good thing it's warm.

Take me home, Ted. He knows just what to do. He matches my pace and keeps his nose forward. Heeling perfectly. Clamber up the noisy metal steps in the rain. Back inside our cozy nook. Back to music and CNN. No zombies jerk-stepping through this beach-town tonite.

Walking Teddy
December Dusk

I walked my dog at 5 one evening. Cold but clear and windless. A few residents in the neighborhood.

Viki Honeywell

Lights coming on in kitchens and on porches. I have not met those people. Who are they? What are they having for dinner? I'm being mindless and mindful. Does that make sense? Nothing urgent. Nothing blue. Just tuning in to little dog breathing and snuffling in dead leaves. He pauses. Does a ballerina leg lift. Then... all done. Come on Mommy, its cold out here. A big fat moon our flashlight tonite. A couple cars on Coastal an easy hum. Kicking gravel both of us just to be raucous. Up the metal steps to bang through our front door. Gittin' us some cozy grub.

Foggy Twos

Today a sheer white curtain cast a sun-washed light on my beach. Treading through its drape, two weathery figures, slow and solid. Bag from Food Lion. They are walking home from a Sunday grocery trip. On the beach. How cute is that? Next are two, one tall, one wee shouting muffled in the wind. Along comes two by two. Daddy Mommy sister dog. Eeking out the last hours of Sunday free before heading off to home across the bridge, to home and homework and sleeping in the car. Our two, Teddy and me, messy and fall downs, nosy in the seagrass and no no leave its, plod through treads and footprints, dropping the leash for a moment's run. Circus dog in dizzy circles. Circus Dog! Circus Dog! Wear yourself out. Now on the foggy end looking south comes beach patrol man. Oops. My pup got loose, Sir. I am very sorry. Won't happen again. Two kindred souls return to our dune, laughing and winking. Teddy and Mommy. Teddy and Me.

Sadie, Sadie

A Poem for Aunt Mary from Teddy and Mommy
Written by Teddy Hoskins with Mommy's Help

Sadie, Sadie was our friend
We loved her sweetness til' the end
Our Sadie's gone, It makes us sad.
But we're so touched by fun we had.
With such a loving and giving heart
She was in ours right from the start
Our Mary had to say good-bye
to Sadie-girl, We all did cry.
But Steve has taken her in to share
The life he has in Heaven there.
Now over the bridge they'll turn to go.
But leaving a secret for us to know
That they are waiting for us to learn
That they'll be there when it's our turn.

I love you,
Aunt Mary!

 32

Potty Training

"Bueller, Bueller...Bueller, Bueller"

IF you recognize this phrase, you are already well on your way to potty training your dog. You will need to take your pup to the designated spot and in the same monotone as the teacher in the movie Ferris Bueller's Day Off, repeat the word Potty, Potty just like that guy said Bueller every few seconds.

Yes, go ahead and try that one out loud. Yeah, right now. I'll give you a moment...

Okay, how did that go for ya? Now try it with Lassie or Buddy or whoever; this may also work with kids. I really have no idea. I don't have any of those.

Kinsey LeBrun

Puppy Math:

*The equations that you will need to know
because your dog refuses to learn the phrase "DROP IT"*

<u>Directions</u> – The first column lists a variety of items that your dog is going to manage to get into his or her very icky petri-dish-like mouth. The second column is a suggested item that you will offer said dirty dog. Depending on your budget, home environment, family, time constraints, dog size and age, you are encouraged to come up with other items that will do that trick. I am not going to do all the work for you. Go get your pencil.

<u>Column One</u>		<u>Column Two</u>
Shoe	=	Other shoe
New Dish Towel	=	Dirty Dish Towel
Paper	=	Better Paper
Arm	=	Rib-eye steak
Sunglasses	=	Dreaded squirt of vinegar water
Ankle with Sock attached	=	Don't even try

Kinsey LeBrun

Dog Monsters

These will scare the living daylights out of your dog and mine. Depends on what your goal is. Just sayin'. Add your monsters to our monsters.

Vacuum cleaner

Broom

Rake

Rug shampooer

Drill

Thunder

Lightening

Garbage Trucks

Skateboards

Metal tape measure

Kinsey LeBrun

Kinsey LeBrun

Test your Treat Sense:

Crunchy or Chewy? Which would you use for each activity?

1. Attempting to put on leash
2. Putting dog clothes on your dog
3. Random barking
4. Your mealtimes

1. Chewy - They take longer to eat and are less messy, so you have a few extra seconds to get that thing on
2. See answer for #1 and why do we do this anyway?
3. See answer for #1 although you theoretically do not give treats for barking, I got so sick of hearing it I gave Teddy a couple gum drops
4. See answer for #1. Slather the floor with peanut butter if you have to, depending on how long you want to be left alone.

Trucie Petty

Glass and Dawgs

Barking at the oven door is cute but obnoxious. Your dog sees his reflection and just wants to play with that dog in there. You can cover it with one of those cheesy magnetic posters from the dollar store. If you want to play a trick on your dog, get one with a different dog on it.

Competition

Does your dog smile? Mine does! I entered Teddy in a dog smile contest with this picture. How could he not win? There were about 20 winners, and some were not even really smiling, sort of grrrr or getting air or breaking wind kinds of faces. Teddy smiles. I told the magazine they were fixing the contest so that their friends' dogs would win. They told me to send them more pictures and they would re-evaluate Teddy's smileability. Re-evaluate? I did. They did. He did not win again. Those Canadian dog magazines... well one Canadian dog magazine. He probably was disqualified because he is, as we know, a DESIGNER dog.

Fun with Food

Throw your dog's dry food all over the kitchen floor. It will take him longer to eat and he will not barf from eating too fast. It will probably give you a cleaner floor too from his tongue. You might also see ants, so this is not a good idea in low-lying areas or basements

Linda Williams

Quiz Time

Do you know why your dog barks at the mailman and the UPS man and the FedEx dude?

        a. They are guys.

        b. They are cute.

        c. They leave.

If you said a. or b. you are needy. If you said c. you are correct. Teddy thinks he is in charge of the neighborhood because he can get the delivery folks to leave when he barks. If I ever decide to date the mailman who I think has a crush on me, we will not be able to go on dates in the mail truck.

Sasha Gardner

Useful Commands

No

NO

NO NO NO

Yes, I realize we are never supposed to say the command more than once but tell that to the dogs. It doesn't work so you just do your no no's until your dog stops whatever it is he is doing. Teddy ate my Invisalign retainer and part of my insulin pump. I had to lie to the company to get a new one without paying the whole price. "Yes, I stepped on it with a hard shoe." I think I lied to my mom too, because I don't think she is wild about Teddy and I did not want to give him a bad rep.

Sharon Bush

Teddy's Vocabulary

Grab your pencil again. Check off the words your dog knows and responds to. Be honest. Let me know if you want me to show you how to teach you any of these.

Sit	_____	Under	_____
Stay	_____	Leave It	_____
Paw	_____	Toothpaste	_____
Paws Up	_____	Run	_____
Up	_____	Kisses	_____
Down	_____	Stop	_____
Off	_____	Wait	_____
Water	_____	Peepee	_____
Beach	_____	Come	_____
Treat	_____	Computer	_____
Acne	_____	Heel	_____
Potty	_____	X-Ray	_____
Ball	_____	Bottle	_____
Toy	_____	Walk	_____
Stranger	_____	Bookbag	_____
Mommy	_____	Leash	_____
Teddy	_____	Underpants	_____
Home	_____	Cupcake	_____
Over	_____	Bed	_____
Covid 19	_____	Hurry	_____

Add commands your dog know that you could teach us!

_____

_____

_____

Nativi-Teddy

All is calm.

All is bright.

The End.

Mary

Baby Jesus

A special thanks to all the artists who made this book happen:

Maria Staub Goebel (My sister, Teddy's aunt)

Kinsey LeBrun

Linda Williams

Trucie Petty (Shane's mom)

Anne Meyers Copeland

Viki Honeywell

Sammy Morgan

Sharon Bush

Sasha Gardner